STEAMING SIXTIES No.11

Ulster Transport Authority
By Terence Dorrity

Copyright Irwell Press,
ISBN-978-1-906919-77-1
First published in 2015 by Irwell Press Ltd., 59A, High
Street, Clophill, Bedfordshire, MK45 4BE
Printed in China

In the 1960s railways in Ireland were run by the Ulster Transport Authority (UTA) in the North and *Córas Iompair Éireann* (CIE) in the Republic. Like British Railways and CIE, the UTA was the result of nationalisation of the railways and it also included bus services and road haulage under its remit. Although obviously not part of British Railways, the UTA network was, in a sense, the United Kingdom's seventh railway region. Two reports before the Second World War had recommended grouping the railways in Ulster but it was not until after the war that this was done. The UTA, which came into existence on 2 September 1948, took control of road services and the Belfast and County Down Railway the following month. The next company to be added was the London Midland and Scottish Railway Northern Counties Committee (NCC) on 1 April 1949. Its parent company, the LMSR, had already been nationalised the previous year as part of British Railways (BR). The last piece of the UTA jigsaw was the Great Northern Railway of Ireland (GNR) which, along with three smaller companies, operated across the border into the Republic of Ireland. The GNR, which had been on the brink of closing its Northern Ireland operations, was run by a joint board, appointed by Dublin and Belfast, from 1 September 1953 until its assets were divided between the nationalised railways on each side of the border in 1958. Northern Ireland even had its version of the notorious Beeching Report. Published in the same year, 1963, the Benson Report recommended the closure of all lines except the ex-GNRI main line from Belfast to Dublin and some local Belfast commuter lines, and the end of freight transport by rail. Much was closed before Northern Ireland Railways was created in 1968 and the UTA was no more.

However, at the time that I took the photographs in this book, in 1963 and 1964, between the publication and implementation of the Benson Report, there was still a lot of railway activity to see and a fleet of steam locomotives that was very much to the British taste. The most numerous NCC locomotives, the WT class 2-6-4Ts and the W class 2-6-0s, clearly showed their LMS Derby roots. The ex-GNR(I) locomotives were of particular interest. A number of them were 4-4-0s, a wheel arrangement that was becoming rare in Britain at the time, and some of them still carried the GNR(I) blue livery and names. Steam locomotives could be seen at the head of local and express passenger services as well as hauling goods trains. There were two busy operational steam sheds in Belfast, at Adelaide and York Road and, among others, a roundhouse at Portadown. It was all shortly to end, but with the pictures in this book we can relive a little the swansong of steam in Ireland.

I would like to thank my mother for taking me to both Dublin and Belfast in 1963. She had the patience to allow me to indulge my interest in railways on what was my first visit to Ireland. We had sailed to Dublin from the Isle of Man and it could have ended badly as, on returning from Inchicore Works, I arrived at the Isle of Man Steam Packet terminal in Dublin just as the ship's gangway was being raised for departure and my mother was desperately trying to persuade the crew to wait a little longer. It was the last ferry of the season to Douglas! Thanks are also due to Michael Collins (yes - really!). I went to Northern Ireland with fellow railway photographer Mike the following year and he has helpfully reminded me of some of the events and locations of that enjoyable trip.

Terence Dorrity, 2015

The nine road ex-Great Northern Railway of Ireland Belfast Adelaide shed on Thursday 26 March 1964, looking very rural with the hills beyond. It remained open until 31 October 1966. Some maintenance was carried out here though Dundalk was the main works in GNR(I) days. Locomotives were turned on a triangle rather than a turntable.

Class V1 0-6-0

No.13X shunting at Belfast Docks Donegall Quay alongside the Heysham shed on Friday 6 September 1963. Ex-NCC No.13X was one of only three LMS Northern Counties Committee V class superheated 0-6-0s built at the LMS Derby Works in 1923. It was rebuilt as a class VI with a Belpaire firebox and new boiler at York Road Works in 1953 The horse-drawn flat wagon belonged to John Harkness and Co which also dealt with heavy haulage and at one time had traction engines in its fleet.

13X shunting alongside the Heysham shed on Friday 6 September 1963. The three goods locomotives of the V class had 5ft 2½in diameter driving wheels and 19in x 24in inside cylinders. The 2,090 gallon capacity six wheeled tender is particularly interesting for its outside springing. The suffix X indicated the locomotive was not permitted on the main line and was restricted to shunting duties. At the time of the photograph it was the sole survivor of its class and it was withdrawn the following year.

Just six months later, on Tuesday 24 March 1964, and looking very sorry for itself, No. 13X stood without its tender at York Road shed. It was not officially withdrawn until August 1964 but it appears it was out of use well before that.

Class SG 0-6-0

No.44, an ex-GNR(I) SG class 0-6-0 (Beyer Peacock 1913, works number 5637) shunting wagons in the yard near Adelaide shed at 2.40pm on Tuesday 24 March 1964. In Great Northern days it was numbered 176. All five of this G.T.Glover designed class were built by Beyer Peacock. The UTA had two of them and the others went to the CIE.

Demonstrating its mixed traffic credentials, No.44 is on a stopping passenger train bound for Belfast Great Victoria Street coming into Adelaide Station down platform on Thursday 26 March 1964. At end of the up platform is the electric signalling recently installed between Belfast and Lisburn, which had come into operation on 2 February.

No.44 a little later that day near Dunmurry, working in the opposite direction on a passenger train towards Portadown. It was withdrawn 1965.

Class SG3 0-6-0

No.37 was yard pilot at Portadown on Wednesday 25 March 1964. It was one of fifteen SG3 class 0-6-0 locomotives built by Beyer Peacock in 1920 and 1921 to a design by G.T.Glover. No.37 was built in 1921 and carried the Beyer Peacock works number 6050. It was originally GNR(I) No.97 and was renumbered as one of eight of the class which became part of the UTA fleet. The ex-GNR(I) 20-ton brake van, No.77, still had the faded letters GN on the side. No.37 was something of a survivor as it passed into NIR ownership and was the last of the class to be scrapped, in 1970, outliving the others by five years.

No.37 at Portadown on Wednesday 25 March 1964. The lines leading off lower right were the coal yard and coal bank sidings. Known as 'Big Ds', the engines were powerful (something approaching the English 4F classification) with 5ft 1in driving wheels and intended for heavy goods working. Apparently, they were funded by the Government as compensation for maintenance arrears incurred during the First World War.

No.34, another SG3 0-6-0, heading light engine for Portadown on Thursday 26 March 1964. Built by Beyer Peacock in 1921 with the works number 6051, its GNR(I) number was 40. It was withdrawn, along with six others of the class, in 1965. It seems that until 1932, when the Boyne Viaduct was strengthened, these heavy locomotives were restricted to working between Belfast and Dundalk and along the 'Derry Road' from Portadown.

Class PGs 0-6-0

No.10X, an ex-GNR(I) PGs class 0-6-0, apparently out of use at Adelaide shed, Belfast, on Friday 6 September 1963. The oldest locomotive in the UTA fleet at the time, it was the last to be built, and the last survivor, of a class of seven introduced in 1899. All were transferred to the UTA. No.10 was built at Dundalk in 1904 (works number 26) and originally carried the name *Bessbrook*. Three of the class, which was designed by Chas Clifford, were constructed by Neilson, Reid & Co of Glasgow and the others by the GNR at Dundalk. They were initially class PG but became class PGs when rebuilt under G.T.Glover with superheated boilers.

Six months later, on Tuesday 24 March 1964, just eleven days before it was sold at auction for scrapping, No10X was at the ex-GNR(I) Maysfield Goods Yard, Belfast (now the site of Belfast Central Station) with its coupling rods already removed. The sad sight of the pile of boiler tubes cut from the carcass of the locomotive behind indicates its inevitable fate. In the background is Belfast Gasworks, near Ormeau Road, which finally closed in 1988. The gasholders have been demolished and the site is now occupied by a business park and the Radisson Blu Hotel.

Class UG 0-6-0

No.45 near Adelaide shed, Belfast, on Friday 6 September 1963. GNR(I) UG class 0-6-0 No.45 was built at Dundalk Works in 1937 with the works number 35. It was originally GNR(I) No.78 but was renumbered when it became part of the UTA fleet. Ten were built, five at Dundalk and five by Beyer Peacock & Co at Gorton, Manchester. Half of the class went to the CIE and half to the UTA. No.45 was withdrawn in 1965.

No.47, another UG class 0-6-0, at the Adelaide shed ash pits on Tuesday 24 March 1964. Like No.45, it was built at Dundalk in 1937 (works number 39) and along with No.45, it was withdrawn in 1965. Its original GNR(I) number was 82.

No.47 shunting goods wagons at Belfast on Thursday 26 March 1964. The class was designed by G.B.Howden, primarily for freight. In contrast to No.45, it had a larger 2,500 gallon Stanier type tender.

No.48 with Stanier-style 2,500 gallon tender, on the turntable at Portadown shed on Wednesday 25 March 1964. It was one of the five slightly more powerful Beyer Peacock UG class 0-6-0s which were built much later than the Dundalk examples, in 1948. No.48 had the works number 7250 and was originally GNR(I) No.146. Portadown shed, a roundhouse built in 1925 in reinforced concrete, was closed the year after this photograph was taken.

Tender-first No.48 on a freight at Portadown on Wednesday 25 March 1964. It was the last of its class to be withdrawn, in 1968, and so outlived the UTA to become part of the NIR (Northern Ireland Railways) fleet.

Class W 2-6-0

No.91 *The Bush*, an ex-LMS Northern Counties Committee W Class 2-6-0, lets off steam at Adelaide shed on Tuesday 24 March 1964. There were fifteen in the class but *The Bush* was one of the first batch of four which were fully constructed at the LMS Derby Works in 1933. It was withdrawn in 1965 and one each of its nameplates and number plates is now displayed at the Irish Transport Museum, Cultra.

The Bush heads the 17:00 Belfast Great Victoria Street to Londonderry Foyle Road passenger train over the Lislea Drive bridge between Adelaide and Balmoral on Tuesday 24 March 1964. It was due to arrive in Derry at 19:55 calling at Portadown, Dungannon, Omagh and Strabane on the way. With their 6ft driving wheels, W Class locomotives often performed on express trains.

The Bush on a passenger train for Belfast near Dunmurry on Thursday 26 March 1964. These two-cylinder locomotives were designed during Stanier's period of office as Chief Mechanical Engineer of the LMS.

Unnamed W Class 2-6-0 No.104 hauls a freight train out of Portadown yard on Wednesday 25 March 1964. This was the very last of the class to be built, in 1942, and was one of eleven assembled at York Road Works from parts supplied by Derby Works. It was withdrawn in 1965. The rear-engined Renault Dauphine on the right adds a bit of Gallic design flair to the scene. Beyond it is a Ford Popular 103E (or possibly the earlier, but similar, Ford Anglia E494A).

No.97 *Earl of Ulster*, assembled at York Road Works in 1935, near Dunmurry on a cross-border train from Dublin Amiens Street to Belfast Great Victoria Street on Thursday 26 March 1964. The train had left Dublin at 09:15 and was due to arrive in Belfast at 12:25. *Earl of Ulster* had recently been fitted with a larger tender for Belfast-Dublin running but would almost certainly have taken over the train from a CIE diesel at Dundalk. No.97 was the last of the class to be withdrawn, at the end of 1965.

Class S2 4-4-0

Adelaide shed, Belfast, was host to No.63 *Slievenamon* on Friday 6 September 1963. This 4-4-0 was ex-Great Northern Railway (Ireland) No. 192, a 'Mountain' class S2 designed by Chas. Clifford and built by Beyer Peacock of Manchester in 1915 with the works number 5903. It was rebuilt with a 175 psi boiler by G.B.Howden at Dundalk in 1938.

Slievenamon at the ex-GNR(I) Adelaide shed, Belfast. These express locomotives had inside 19in x 26in cylinders and 6ft 7in driving wheels. Named after a 2,365ft mountain in County Tipperary, *Slievenamon* was withdrawn in 1965.

Sister S2 'Mountain' 4-4-0 No.62 *Lugnaquilla*, named after the 3,035ft peak in County Wicklow, inside Adelaide shed on Tuesday 24 March 1964. The loco was ex-GNR No.190, built by Beyer Peacock in 1915 with the works number 5901. Like *Slievenamon* it was rebuilt by G.B.Howden at Dundalk, in this case in 1939, and it was withdrawn in 1965. Three of the class were built for the GNR(I) in 1915; the third, *Croaghpatrick*, became part of the CIE fleet and was withdrawn much earlier, in 1960.

Class S 4-4-0

No.174 *Carrantuohill* stored by the turntable at the ex-LMS-NCC Belfast York Road Works on Tuesday 24 March 1964. It was an ex-GNR(I) S class 4-4-0 designed by Chas. Clifford, built by Beyer Peacock in 1913 with the works number 5632 and rebuilt by G.B.Howden. Named after the 3,123ft mountain in County Kerry, Ireland's highest, it was one of a class of five and had gone to the CIE, along with two others, on the division of the GNR(I). It was bought by the UTA in 1963 and retained its Great Northern blue livery. It was withdrawn in 1965.

Class S 4-4-0 No.170 *Errigal* at Adelaide Shed, Belfast, in the early afternoon of Tuesday 24 March 1964. Like *Carrantuohill,* it too was bought from the CIE in 1963 and remained in blue. It was built by Beyer Peacock in 1913 with the works number 5628 and was withdrawn not much more than a year after this photograph was taken, in May 1965. The carriage, N382, was ex-GNR(I) No.172, a K13 type 68 seat third class corridor vehicle built in 1932.

No.170 *Errigal* crosses the Lislea Drive bridge between Adelaide and Balmoral on the 17:40 Belfast to Dungannon train on Tuesday 24 March 1964. Balmoral signal box, which had controlled the sidings for the Royal Ulster Agricultural Society (RUAS) showgrounds but had recently been closed, can be seen in the distance. The trace of the recently lifted third line which ran to the showground sidings is very evident. Errigal is a 2,464ft peak in County Donegal.

Errigal passes with the same train. The newly installed electric signalling, which had come into operation on 2 February, can be seen ahead. In August 1935, as an echo of the GWR and LNER exchanges ten years earlier, *Errigal* was involved in a locomotive exchange with NCC W class 2-6-0 No.96 *Silver Jubilee*. The carriage, N483, was ex-GNR(I) No.377, a D4 type non-corridor brake/80 second class seat vehicle classified as type E3 when built in 1921.

Travelling in the opposite direction shortly afterwards, passing R. E. Hamilton Main Ford Dealer's Lislea Drive building in Belfast between Balmoral and Adelaide stations, class S 4-4-0 No.171 *Slieve Gullion*, also in GNR(I) blue, heads the 15:45 Omagh to Belfast Great Victoria Street train. It was the third of the class bought from the CIE in 1963. It was originally built by Beyer Peacock in 1913, with the works number 5629, and was rebuilt at Dundalk Works in 1938. The redundant semaphore signal arms have already been removed as has the third line to the RUAS showground goods platforms and sidings. Interestingly, this engine features on two 1985 Grenadines of St Vincent 50c stamps!

Class S 4-4-0 No.60 *Slieve Donard* approaches Portadown on a goods train on Wednesday 25 March 1964. Originally GNR(I) No. 172, it was one of two of the class which went directly to the UTA on the break up of the Great Northern in 1958. It was joined by the other three of the class which were bought from the CIE in 1963. The two locomotives that had gone directly to the UTA, unlike the others, had been repainted in UTA lined black. Built by Beyer Peacock in 1913, with the works number 5630, *Slieve Donard* was withdrawn in 1965.

Later that day *Slieve Donard* was in Portadown goods yard. The signal box in the distance controlled the complicated junction of three lines: the Derry Road to the right, the line to Dundalk and Dublin to the left and, in the middle, a short section of the closed Armagh line allowing access to a factory. There were also points leading to the roundhouse engine shed and sidings from the latter two lines. This locomotive was named after the highest mountain in Ulster, at 2,790ft one of the Mountains of Mourne in County Down.

On the following day, Thursday 26 March 1964, *Slieve Donard* was on the ash pits at Adelaide Shed. I believe it was allocated to Londonderry shed at this time and until the closure of the 'Derry Road' the following year. S class Nos.171 and 172 (60) were experimentally fitted for oil firing in 1936 but were re-converted to coal burning by the end of the year and substantially rebuilt two years later at Dundalk Works under a programme which included all five of the class.

No.171 *Slieve Gullion* catches the evening light after passing Lambeg station on a train from Belfast on Wednesday 25 March 1964. *Slieve Gullion* fared better than the others of its class as it is now with the Railway Preservation Society of Ireland. According to the RPSI website, it was leased from Northern Ireland Railways (NIR) from New Year's Day 1966 for £40 per annum, with the option to buy at a later date. In 1968 it was overhauled in Belfast at the Harland & Wolff shipyard at a cost of £2,750. Its more recent overhaul took it to England to Rail Restorations North East Ltd in Shildon, County Durham. It is named after the 1,880ft mountain in County Armagh.

No.170 *Errigal* approaching Adelaide Road station with the York Road breakdown train on Thursday 26 March 1964, on the way to an incident at Portadown shed where 0-6-0 SG2 class No.38 had rolled into the turntable pit during the night. The floodlights in the background are at Windsor Park stadium where the following month, on 19th April, the seventeen-year old George Best, wearing a green No.7 shirt, played in his first international Northern Ireland home match, against Uruguay. It resulted in a 3-0 victory for Northern Ireland.

Later that day, *Errigal* returns to Belfast on the breakdown train after retrieving the locomotive from the Portadown turntable pit. The 36-ton York Road steam breakdown crane was built for the NCC by Cowans Sheldon and Co in 1931. It is now to be found in preservation on the Downpatrick and County Down Railway, County Down.

Class U 4-4-0

No.66 *Meath*, an ex-GNR(I) U class 4-4-0 built by Beyer Peacock in January 1948 with the works number 7244, prepares to leave platform four at Belfast Great Victoria Street Station on Wednesday 25 March 1964. The bus is on what had once been the adjacent platform five. The imposing GNR(I) terminus was demolished in the 1970s and the site is now occupied by the Europa Hotel (much in the news during the 'Troubles') along with the coach station and, with at least a nod to history, the Great Northern Mall. The present platforms start under the Boyne Bridge which was officially inaugurated on 18 December 1936. There is still a bus depot alongside.

No.66 *Meath* by the carriage sheds at Belfast on Thursday 26 March 1964. It originally carried the Great Northern Railway of Ireland number 201. Five of these U class locomotives were built, all by Beyer Peacock, to a development by McIntosh which was closely based on an earlier, 1915, Glover-designed U class. *Meath* was withdrawn in May 1965.

No.67 *Louth*, another ex-GNR(I) U class 4-4-0, trundles past tender-first on a mixed goods train bound for Belfast, through typically attractive countryside near Dunmurry on Thursday 26 March 1964. The gently sloping Colin Mountain rises directly behind the locomotive. The flat wagon is carrying an Inglis Belfast bakery bread container. *Louth* could not be turned at Portadown depot because of a derailment.

On the same day a little time later *Louth* was returning in the opposite direction just past Dunmurry on a Belfast to Portadown passenger train. *Louth* was built by Beyer Peacock in January 1948 with the works number 7245. Originally GNR(I) No. 202, it became UTA No.67 in 1958 and it was withdrawn in May 1965. On the break up of the GNR(I) in 1958 three U class 4-4-0s went to the UTA and two to the CIE.

Class VS 4-4-0

No.58 *Lagan* inside Adelaide shed Belfast on Tuesday 24 March 1964. One of five handsome GNR(I) VS class 4-4-0 three cylinder express locomotives designed by H.R. McIntosh that were the most powerful GNR(I) express engines. Unusually, for Ireland, were fitted with smoke deflectors. They were built in 1948 by Beyer Peacock for use on Belfast to Dublin expresses. No.58 *Lagan* was ex-GNR(I) number 208 and had the works number 6963. it was withdrawn in May 1965.

VS class 4-4-0 No.207 *Boyne* was also inside the nine road Adelaide shed that day. On the break-up of the GNR(I) it went, with two others, to the CIE but was bought by the UTA in 1963 to join the two VS locomotives that they already had. It was built by Beyer Peacock in 1948 (works number 6962); like *Lagan*, *Boyne* was withdrawn on 21 May 1965 so it had a very short life with the UTA.

Class Z 0-6-4T

No.27 *Lough Erne* was, and fortunately still is, an ex-Sligo, Leitrim and Northern Counties Railway 0-6-4 tank. Shunting at the Belfast Harbour Commission Docks on Tuesday 24 March 1964, it was one of two built by Beyer Peacock in 1949 and carried the works number 7242. They were given numbers and the classification class Z by the UTA. Prior to that, they had carried only names. The car is a 1953 Morris Oxford. The PZ registration was issued by the Belfast DVA licensing office from January 1953 to August 1954.

Lough Erne the same day; along with its sister *Lough Melvin,* it was ready for delivery when new to the SL&NCR but, apparently, the railway company was unable to pay for them. After two years in store in England, they were sent to Ireland under a leasing agreement but as they were still not fully paid for when the SL&NCR closed in 1957 Beyer Peacock took charge of them once again. Another two years passed before they were auctioned and bought by the UTA, in December 1959, for £700 each.

When No.27 *Lough Erne* was withdrawn in 1969 it was bought for preservation and is now at the Railway Preservation Society of Ireland's base at Whitehead. This has enabled it to outlive the ship 'Colytto' which was built in Bergen, Norway, and launched in 1957. At the time of this photograph 'Colytto' was registered to a Dutch company in Rotterdam but it was sold on to a Greek shipping company in 1967. It ran aground on the East African coast in May 1972 en route from Mombasa to Lourenço Marques and was broken up on the spot.

No.26 *Lough Melvin,* the other ex-SL&NCR Beyer Peacock 1949-built Z class 0-6-4T (works number 7138) in front of 4-4-0 No.67 *Louth* at Belfast Adelaide shed on 24 March 1964. Withdrawn in 1967, *Lough Melvin* was scrapped the following year. The Z class had 18x24in cylinders and 4ft 8in driving wheels.

Class T1 4-4-2T

No.187X, the last survivor of the T1 class 4-4-2 tanks, inside Adelaide shed, Belfast, on Friday 6 September 1963. It was one of five built for Belfast and Dublin suburban services by Beyer Peacock at Gorton, Manchester, for the GNR(I) in 1913 to a design by G.T.Glover. No.187X carried the works number 5737. When the GNR(I) stock was divided up four went to the UTA and only one to the CIE. The X suffix, as mentioned earlier, meant a locomotive was not permitted on the main line and was restricted to shunting duties; moreover it heralded an early demise, for there would be no more major repairs for such locomotives.

With GNR on its tanks to the end, No.187X stands forlornly at the ex-GNR(I) Maysfield Goods Yard, Belfast (now the site of Belfast Central Station) on Tuesday 24 March 1964, just eleven days before it was sold at auction for scrapping. The T1 tanks had 18x24in cylinders and, when built, saturated boilers. They were later modified with superheaters.

Class T2 4-4-2T

No.5X, a class T2 4-4-2 tank locomotive, awaits its fate at the ex GNR Maysfield Goods Yard, Belfast on Thursday 26 March 1964, just two months before it was sold for scrap. Like the T1 No.187X, this was the last survivor of a class which consisted of twenty superheated locomotives. It had probably outlived the others because of its role as a station pilot at Belfast Great Victoria Street station during its final years. The T2s were a modified version of the T1 and also designed by G.T.Glover. They were built by Nasmyth Wilson of Patricroft, Salford, and Beyer Peacock, from 1921 to 1930. On the demise of the Great Northern, nine went to the UTA and eleven to the CIE. No.5X was built for the GNR(I) by Beyer Peacock in 1921 with the works number 6039.

Class WT 2-6-4T

Known as 'Jeeps' by the railwaymen, the ex NCC Derby produced WT class parallel boiler 2-6-4 locomotives were introduced in 1946. Eighteen examples of this tank engine version of the 2-6-0 W class were built, first by the London Midland and Scottish Railway and then, after it was nationalised, by British Railways. No.54, a BR 1950 product, was on Adelaide shed, Belfast, on Friday 6 September 1963. It was withdrawn in February 1970.

Oiling WT 2-6-4T No.6 while partly on the turntable at Belfast York Road shed at nine o'clock on the very wet morning of Tuesday 24 March 1964. This locomotive was built by the LMS at Derby in 1946. It was withdrawn from service in 1970.

A WT class locomotive waits at Portadown station with a morning train to Belfast on Wednesday 25 March 1964. The carriage, N312, was ex-GNR(I) K7 type corridor 'tea car' No.41 built in 1914 but converted to fully third class seating in 1948. The 12-ton goods van, No.2408, was an ex-LMS-NCC 2400 type fitted vehicle. These were often attached to passenger trains to convey parcels. The roof of the signal box at the end of the island platform can be seen beyond the van.

WT No.56 leaves Portadown on Wednesday 25 March 1964 at the head of the cross border 09:15 Dublin Amiens Street (now Connolly) station to Belfast Great Victoria Street station, where it was due to arrive at 12:25. Portadown station is in the background and to its left the prominent tower of Saint Mark's Church, rebuilt in 1928 as a war memorial to those killed in the First World War. No.56, built in 1950, was withdrawn in 1970.

About three hours later, WT 2-6-4T No.57 approached Portadown on a cross-border train in the opposite direction which had left Great Victoria Street at 14:15 and was due to arrive at Dublin Amiens Street station at 17:05. The carriages belonged to the Irish Republic *Córas Iompair Éireann* (CIE). Some of them were in the new orange and black livery, others in the older ivy green with a white band. No.57 had been seen on York Road shed the previous day. It was the last of the Derby WT class to be built, in 1950, and it was withdrawn in 1968.

WT class No.1 was also at Portadown on Wednesday 25 March 1964 showing that these engines were equally at home on goods, expresses or local passenger trains. They had 6ft driving wheels. The two outside cylinders were 19in x 26in stroke and their weight in working order was 87½ tons. They had self-cleaning smokeboxes, rocking grates and self emptying ashpans. No.1, obviously the first of the WT class to be built, in 1947, was withdrawn at the same time as the last one, No.57, in 1968.

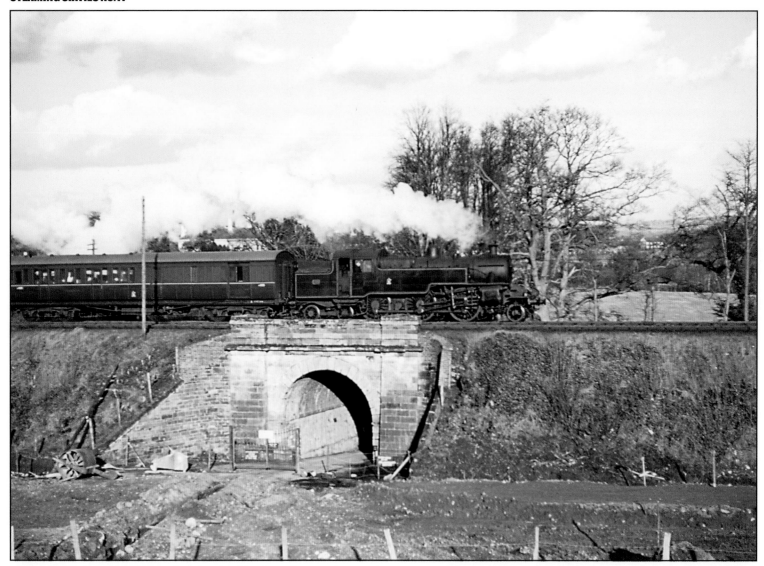

Class WT No.7 crosses the Lambeg Road bridge just after Lambeg station on an evening commuter train from Belfast on Wednesday 25 March 1964. It was built at Derby in 1947 and, like its sisters 1 and 57, was withdrawn in 1968. Work on widening the Queensway had just started.

A class WT 2-6-4 tank on an evening train to Belfast easily overtakes a Ford Popular 103E as it approaches Lambeg on Wednesday 25 March 1964, just five days after the Parlophone 7 inch Beatles 'Can't Buy me Love' was released.

WT 2-6-4T No. 5 passes near Dunmurry on the 14:15 cross-border train from Belfast Great Victoria Street station to Dublin Amiens Street station, where it was due to arrive at 17:05, on Thursday 26 March 1964. The locomotive would almost certainly have followed the practice of the time and handed over this train to a CIE diesel at Dundalk. There were, strangely, two weekday stopping trains from Belfast to Dublin and three in the other direction. The balancing turn was an early morning newspaper train. No.5 was built at Derby in 1956 and withdrawn in October 1970.

WT class No.4, built at Derby in 1947, pulls away from York Road on a goods train at five past nine in the morning on Tuesday 24 March 1964. This photograph was taken from the footbridge which crossed the line from Duncrue Street Works. To the right is the shed yard with its water towers, with lines leading to the coaling plant, locomotive shed and railcar sheds. No.4 was one of the WT class retained to haul spoil trains on the Larne line after most steam had been withdrawn. It was not retired until mid-1971, almost three years after the famous British Railways end of steam '15 guinea special' in August 1968.

No.4, twenty-four years later at Dublin Connolly Station (the old Amiens Street) demonstrates that steam lives on in Ireland thanks to the Railway Preservation Society of Ireland (RPSI). It was on the Boyne Special which ran from Connolly to Drogheda and Navan and back on Saturday 27 August 1988. The then four-year old NIR Canadian-built General Motors diesel electric Co-Co No.113 is alongside on a regular Belfast train. No.4 was one of the small number of the 2-6-4Ts retained in service to haul motorway construction spoil trains. Most of the class were withdrawn either in 1968 or in 1970 but No.4, along with two other survivors, Nos.51 and 53, continued in service until 1971 when it was bought by the RPSI. It is now based at their centre at Whitehead, County Antrim.

Guiness 0-4-0 saddle tank

A brief excursion into the Republic for Guinness Dublin Brewery Hudswell Clarke 0-4-0ST No.3 (works number 1152 of 1919) with sister locomotive No.2 (Hudswell Clarke 1914, works number 1079) on Wednesday 4 September 1963. These locomotives were used to take transfer traffic between the brewery and Dublin Heuston station (at the time known as Kingsbridge station) and for safety reasons while street working both had brass bells and enclosed wheels and motion. Rail transfer to the CIE ended on 15 May 1965 and No.2 was scrapped soon afterwards.

No.3 became the first locomotive to be preserved by the Railway Preservation Society of Ireland when it was presented to them on withdrawal from service in 1965 and it is now to be found at their Whitehead site. Though clearly not in service in Northern Ireland, these photos have been included because the CIE ceased using steam locomotives in regular service at the end of 1962 and so these saddle tanks, and a few side tanks operated by *Cómhlucht Siúicre Éireann*, the Irish Sugar Corporation, represent the only 5ft 3in gauge steam locomotives still in regular use in the Republic at the time.

Class B1a 4-6-0

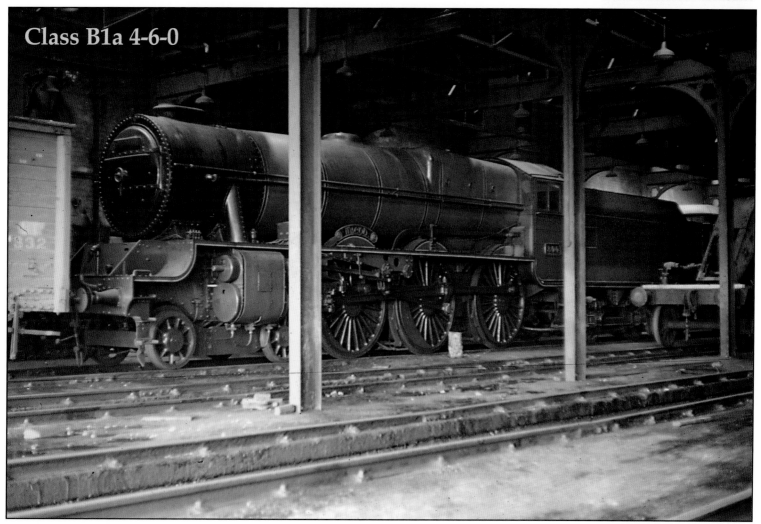

The impressive 3-cylinder 4-6-0 class B1a No.800 *Maeve/Maebdh*, built in 1939, inside Adelaide depot on Tuesday 24 March 1964. Three of these E.C.Bredin designed locomotives were built at the Great Southern Railway's Inchicore Works to haul express trains between Dublin and Cork. This locomotive had been withdrawn by the CIE in 1962. It had a relatively short stay at Adelaide, where it had arrived on 28 February, as it was on its way to the old Belfast Whitham Street Transport Museum. There was a ceremonial handover at Great Victoria Street station on 16 April. It is now to be found at the Ulster Folk and Transport Museum in Cultra.

Class JT 2-4-2T

At this time several steam locomotives were already inside the rather cramped old Belfast Whitham Street Transport Museum. Among them, on Wednesday 25 March 1964, was Great Northern Railway (Ireland) JT class 2-4-2 tank No.93. Originally named *Sutton*, it was built at Dundalk Works in 1895 with the works number 16. Six of the class, designed by J.C.Park but introduced after his death, were built there between 1895 and 1902. They were primarily intended for use on Dublin suburban services but later they could be found on branch lines. No.93 was withdrawn in 1955 and only one, No.91, outlived the GNR(I) to be withdrawn by the CIÉ in 1963. Like *Maeve/Maebdh*, it is now in the museum at Cultra.